Once in a lifetime...
LEAF

an "I believe in you" book

Written by Marietta Camps

Illustrated by Yana Zybina

First Published in Ontario, Canada in 2018
by www.duo.ca

enquiries: ncamps@duo.ca
© 2018 Marietta Camps

Once in a lifetime...
LEAF

an "I believe in you" book

Written by Marietta Camps

Illustrated by Yana Zybina

The forest was ablaze with fall colours and the leaves were whispering amongst themselves, when a gust of wind sighed through the branches and sent them twirling and spinning to the forest floor, soon to be followed by others until there was only one solitary leaf left.

"Come down, come down!" cried the leaves as they made themselves comfortable in the moist earth below. But the leaf remained stubbornly attached to his branch.

"Don't you wish to join your friends?" encouraged a puzzled Wind.

"I first want to have an adventure," replied Leaf, clinging on for dear life. Nearby, an acorn wisely nodded its little capped head.

"Alright," said Wind. "You shall have your adventure, but your end will remain the same."

"Fine," answered Leaf. "I shall take the chance, but an adventure I must have."

So Wind huffed and puffed and Leaf let go and sailed away on Wind's breath, up, up and over the great forest, over hills and meadows, over lakes and rivers until they came to a wide and noisy highway with cars and trucks going at high speed in every direction.

"Don't drop me, don't drop me!"

cried a frightened Leaf as Wind slowed and drifted into the moving traffic and gently deposited the shaking leaf on to a fast-moving truck.

"Rest now and don't worry, you won't be blown off because I have you safely wedged between these boxes," and with that, Wind disappeared and Leaf was left to himself.

At first, it scared him to be so alone, but after a while, he began to look about him. The truck sped on and on, past fields and meadows, hills and valleys.

It was growing dark and Leaf, curled up in his little corner, began to feel lonely, wondering if he had made a mistake in not joining his companions on the forest floor.

"Where am I going and where is my adventure and what if Wind does not come back for me!"

But before he could think of an answer, he fell fast asleep, curled comfortably in his corner. He slept through the night and never once work up. He didn't know that all the trucks had stopped moving and their drivers had disappeared into a friendly restaurant for a meal and a night's rest.

It was still very dark and a
reluctant Sun had not yet shown its face
when Leaf was woken up by Wind,
which whistled and tugged,

"Wake up, wake up, time to go on your adventure!"

"Where are we going?" asked a still-sleepy Leaf as he whirled and twirled along with the impatient Wind.

"To a big city," replied Wind.

"What is a city?" asked Leaf, but Wind just blew stronger and stronger and Leaf had no choice but to go along.

After a while, he noticed that the traffic was getting busier, and that there were fewer trees and fields and more buildings, some small, some large and some quite ugly.

"Where are we?"
asked Leaf, huffing and puffing as he raced along.

"In the city,"

answered Wind and then blew so hard that within a second, Leaf found himself on the ledge of the tallest building of them all, which, explained Wind, was called a skyscraper.

Leaf saw buildings and more buildings below with what seemed like ants crawling in between them.

But before he could ask Wind what they were, Wind had swooped him up, and down they blew, down to the pavement and sidewalk, where they were joined by old newspapers and rubbish that Wind picked up in passing...

Just then, he was blown against a large window and Leaf was amazed at what he saw inside! It was a jeweller's shop, and it seemed that hundreds and hundreds of eyes were blinking back at him.

"Much more to see," whistled Wind and with a swoop, scooped him up and rushed him here, there, and everywhere, past every store you could imagine. Toy shops, bicycle shops, bakeries, smart dress shops and what Leaf liked best of all, a flower shop and for a brief moment, he thought he could smell his forest again.

By this time Leaf was beginning to look a bit bedraggled. He had lost his beautiful red fall colours and he was a bit ragged along the edges. In fact, he had become a dull brown with a few little holes here and there. Wind had of course noticed, and he blew a little more gently and rested more often, now on a statue in a park along with a roosting pigeon or in a quiet little corner of a doorway.

"Now for the last part
 of your adventure,
  little leaf," said Wind,

and with a huff and a puff, blew him over a large lake, skimming over boats with their sails puffed out or teasing Leaf over choppy waves so that he was afraid that he would sink forever into the deep waters.

But Leaf was getting very tired and Wind whispered kindly,
 "Where would you like to end this adventure, little leaf?"

"In a forest, please,"

answered Leaf, utterly exhausted.

"Right!" whistled Wind and blew the leaf back over the land, buildings and sidewalks, over the heads of the city's people into a quiet, deep forest.

"Aaah!
I am at home,"
were Leaf's last thoughts as he fluttered down to the forest floor.

"Goodbye, goodbye little leaf," whispered Wind, but Leaf did not hear him, for he was fast asleep.

Nature is yours to protect

Long before houses, roads and tall buildings were built by people, the earth was covered by forests, meadows, streams, lakes, rivers, oceans and even deserts. We call this nature. It's good for us to learn about nature in order to protect it, because nature is very important to the way we live. **Let's think about one part of nature… trees.**

A collection of trees is called a stand. A large stand of trees is called a forest. The tallest branches and leaves in a forest is called a canopy. The canopy is what you see when you go into a forest and look way up.

A forest is much more than the trees you see. Do you know some of the important things trees do?

1. Trees are home to birds and animals. For example, owls live in holes high up in trees. Many animals find shelter in spaces under tree roots, in holes in trees and on tree branches.

2. Trees give us protection by providing shade on a hot day or by blocking wind and cold.

3. A long, long time ago, people used trees for so many things. People built houses, furniture, musical instruments and ships from trees and it was also used to provide heat in stoves. A tree that is cut down gives us wood. We call this wood lumber. When cutting down trees for lumber or firewood, it is important to know which trees to cut and which trees not to cut. This is called forest stewardship. You can study forest stewardship in school.

4. Trees and their leaves clean our air which is especially important in cities where cars and factories pollute the air. Trees and plants remove pollutants from the air by absorbing unhealthy gases through their leaves and roots. The air that people breathe out is what trees and plants need to take in, and the air that plants and trees put out is necessary for people to breathe in. People and plants and trees are interdependent, meaning one needs the other in order to survive. Do you have plants inside where you live? They could be making fresh air for you to breathe.

5. Trees feed most of what lives in nature. The nuts that fall from trees are food for many animals. A tree produces leaves which are sometimes eaten by animals and caterpillars. Some leaves can be used as food and medicine for people.

6. Trees have roots that spread into the earth, keeping the tree upright. Those same roots keep the soil around the roots from rushing away in a big rainfall, which could cause flooding in towns and cities.

7. Did you know that you can plant trees yourself? For example, you can find acorns on the ground in the fall wherever oak trees grow. An acorn is a nut with what looks like a little hat - or sometimes the hat has fallen off. Soak your acorns in water overnight. In the next day or so, plant your acorns outside just below the surface and cover with dirt. You will be growing an oak tree! Once your acorn takes root it will grow the height of this book every year. Imagine that when you are much, much, much older, you can look over at an oak tree and know that you were the one who planted it. Many people plant trees that have already been growing for several years; these trees are called saplings and they are purchased at a place called a nursery.

8. Being with trees in a forest provides a feeling of happiness and calm. Ask your parents or caregiver to take you for a walk in the forest. Look down at the roots of a tree. Look way up to the canopy of the forest. Listen to the birds who are on the branches of the trees. Look at all the different kinds of trees by looking at their leaves. See the page in this book that shows you the leaves and needles belonging to some trees found in Canada.

9. In Canada we have four separate seasons. Winter, spring, summer and fall. This story took place in the fall. You know it's fall because the leaves were all changing colour and then falling to the forest floor. In winter, the trees have no leaves and we can see the trunk and branches clearly. In spring, the leaves first appear as little buds that open into leaves. Summer is a time for leaves to give us shade.

Notice nature. Learn about nature on your own by reading books. Think about studying nature in school. Walk in nature and notice all the different trees, plants and living creatures.

Protect nature and it will work hard for you whether you live in the country or in the city. Cities need nature in order to be healthy places for people. Both city and country spaces need help keeping nature safe.

Being in nature is a wonderful adventure for everyone.